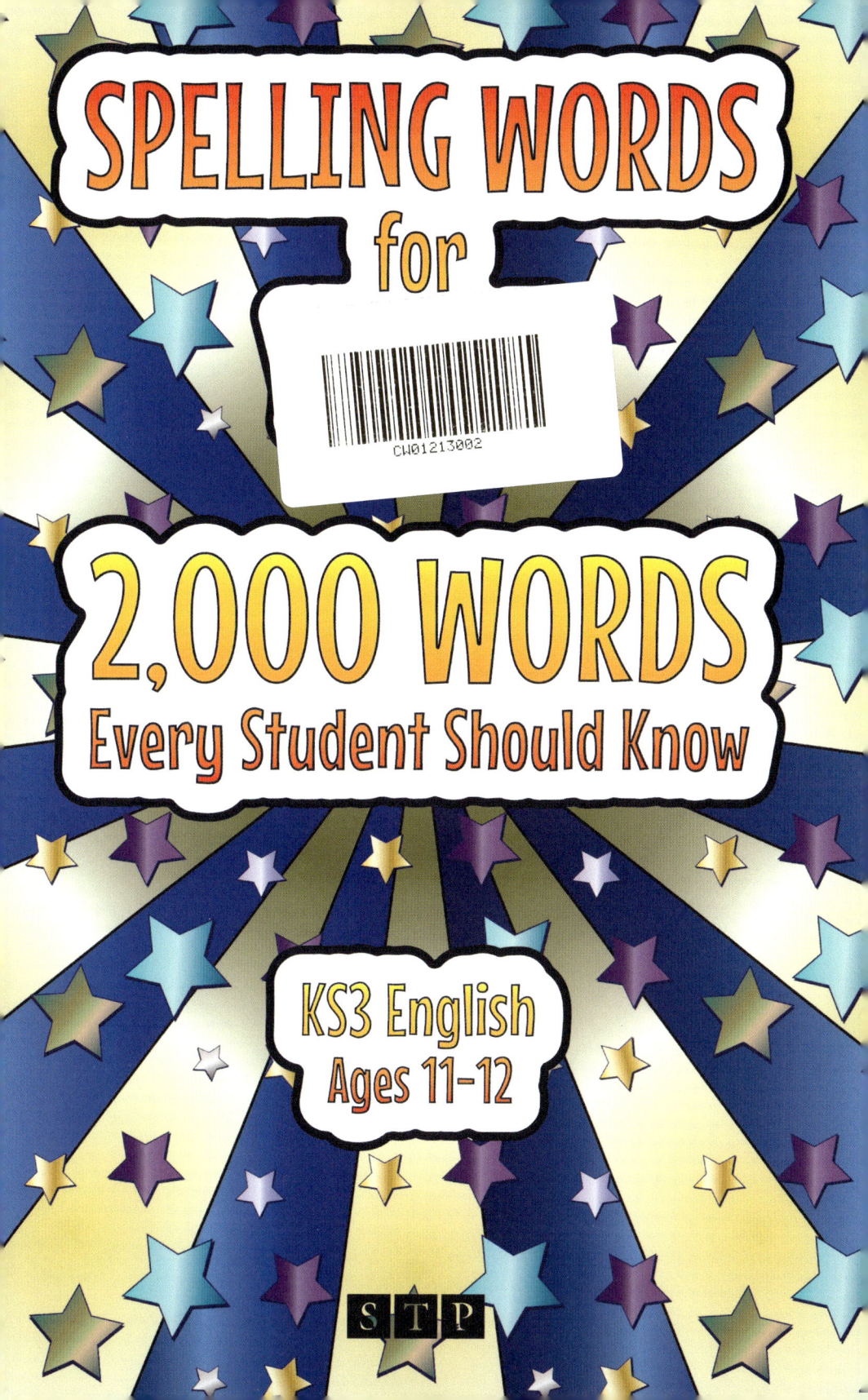

ABOUT THIS BOOK

Using a **fresh approach** to spellings lists, this illustrated collection of Spelling Words is designed **to make spelling fun** for students whilst ensuring they master essential spelling rules by the end of Year 7.

Containing **2,000** carefully selected **level-appropriate** words, this book is made up of **70** Themed Spellings Lists that

- Have **brightly-coloured illustrated backgrounds** and **engaging titles**
- Cover **loads of topics** that **actually interest students** such as Cinema & Film, Pirates, and Video Games
- Relate to other **areas covered at school** like chemistry, the Middle Ages, and Shakespearean English
- Target **key words that students overuse** (e.g. 'walk', 'easy', and 'said')
- Quietly introduce **specific areas of spelling** that students need to know (e.g. word building, using prefixes and suffixes, and hyphenating adjectives)
- Are made up of **25 to 30 words each**

HOW TO USE IT

All the **lists are self-contained**, so you can work through them **in order**, or, you can dip in to use them for **focused practice**. And, as these lists are themed, they are **also a useful resource** for a range of **writing projects and exercises**.

For your convenience, an **Index** to the **spelling rules, patterns, and themed areas** dealt with by each of the lists is included at the **back of the book** on page 40.

Published by STP Books
An imprint of Swot Tots Publishing Ltd
Kemp House
152-160 City Road
London EC1V 2NX

www.swottotspublishing.com

Text, design, illustrations and layout © Swot Tots Publishing Ltd
First published 2020

Swot Tots Publishing Ltd have asserted their moral right under the Copyright, Designs and Patents Act, 1988, to be identified as the author of this work.

All rights reserved. Without limiting the rights under copyright reserved above, no part of this publication may be reproduced, stored in a retrieval system, or transmitted in any form or by any means electronic, mechanical, photocopying, printing, recording, or otherwise without either the prior permission of the publishers or a licence permitting restricted copying in the United Kingdom issued by the Copyright Licensing Agency Limited, 5th Floor, Shackleton House, Hay's Galleria, 4 Battle Bridge Lane, London SE1 2HX.

Typeset, cover design, and inside concept design by Swot Tots Publishing Ltd.

British Library Cataloguing-in-Publication Data. A catalogue record for this book is available from the British Library.

ISBN 978-1-912956-29-6

Ye Olde English	5	Happy Endings III	14
Double Trouble	5	Ancient Origins	14
Happy Endings I	6	The Age Of Chivalry?	15
In One's Element	6	Bygone Days	15
All That Glitters...	7	Sound Effects	16
That's Just Plain Silly!	7	Light Effects	16
Spoilt For Choice I	8	That Doesn't Look Right...	17
De- The Decoded	8	On The Road	17
The Game Is Afoot!	9	Fasten Your Seat Belt!	18
Dead Easy Or Uphill Battle?	9	In Good Company	18
Mad Scientists	10	From A Great Height	19
H Is For Hospital	10	Where There's Smoke...	19
Happy Endings II	11	On Or Off The Cards?	20
What's Cooking?	11	Spoilt For Choice II	20
5-A-Day	12	Blue Rhymes With...	21
Q Is For...	12	Nessing Things Up	21
They Asked, We Replied	13	Pirates!!	22
En- The Enriched	13	Well- The Well-Fed	22

CONTENTS Cont.

Ill- The Ill-Informed	23
How Awful!	23
Measuring Up	24
And The Winner Is...	24
All Shapes And Sizes	25
Loanwords	25
Under- The Underlined	26
Drip...Drip...Drip	26
Gruesome Grammar	27
The Silver Screen	27
Isn't It Crystal Clear?	28
Friend...	28
...Or Foe?	29
There's No Going Back	29
Retreat! Retreat!	30
Sherlock Holmes & Co.	30
City Central	31
Bookish Business	31
Left, Right, Left, Right...	32
Acting Your Age	32
Un- The Unheeded	33
The Big Top	33
Dotting I's & Crossing T's	34
What's It Worth?	34
Open For Business	35
'Ch' Is For 'Chaos'	35
On The Face Of It	36
Art For Art's Sake	36
A Splash Of Colour	37
Out- The Outnumbered	37
Upstairs & Downstairs	38
Bad Hair Day?	38
Player 1 Is Ready	39
That's A Proper Word?!	39
Index	40

Ye Olde English

abhor	hast	thou
anon	hie	thy
art	hither	vain
assay	knave	wast
aught	moiety	wert
canst	sans	whence
dost	shalt	wherefore
doth	thee	wilt
fain	thine	ye
hark	thither	yea

Double Trouble

accommodate	efficacy	tattoo
accuse	ellipse	territory
ambassador	erroneous	tomorrow
apparel	essence	utterance
appointment	gallantry	warranty
attached	gimmick	
attendees	occult	
bulletins	offence	
colloquial	syllabus	
currency	symmetry	

Happy Endings I

acreage	patronage	tonnage
breakage	percentage	tutelage
coverage	pilgrimage	voltage
drainage	postage	wastage
heritage	sabotage	wreckage
leverage	seepage	
lineage	slippage	
mileage	spillage	
orphanage	stoppage	
outage	storage	

In One's Element

argon	helium	radium
arsenic	hydrogen	silicon
barium	iodine	sulphur
beryllium	krypton	xenon
boron	lithium	zirconium
cadmium	manganese	
calcium	neon	
carbon	nitrogen	
chlorine	oxygen	
fluorine	phosphorus	

All That Glitters...

aluminium	magnesium	tin
brass	mercury	titanium
bronze	nickel	tungsten
chromium	pewter	uranium
cobalt	platinum	zinc
copper	plutonium	
electrum	potassium	
gold	silver	
iron	sodium	
lead	steel	

That's Just Plain Silly!

absurd	hare-brained	ridiculous
asinine	idiotic	risible
barmy	inane	senseless
brainless	irrational	stupid
daft	irresponsible	unreasonable
farcical	laughable	
far-fetched	ludicrous	
foolhardy	nonsensical	
foolish	outrageous	
frivolous	preposterous	

Spoilt For Choice 1

acidic	drab	homely
ajar	excruciating	hushed
antiquated	exorbitant	immersive
avaricious	feisty	intrepid
bountiful	forked	intricate
canopied	frail	opaque
cavernous	grandiose	reflective
compassionate	grimy	searing
deafening	grotesque	spartan
distorted	hoarse	turbulent

De- The Decoded

deactivate	deforest	depopulate
debrief	defrost	depreciate
decapitate	degrade	deregulate
decelerate	dehumanise	deselect
declassify	dehumidify	destabilise
decode	dehydrate	detach
decompose	delineate	dethrone
decompress	demoralise	detract
deflate	demystify	devalue
deflect	denounce	devolve

The Game Is Afoot!

ambush	devour	quarry
beast	exhaust	scavenger
bloodshed	feral	snare
butchery	ferret	stalk
cadaver	omnivore	swoop
carcass	pounce	
carnage	predator	
carnivore	prey	
carrion	prowl	
corpse	pursuit	

Dead Easy Or Uphill Battle?

cinch	unchallenging	exacting
doable	uncomplicated	exhausting
effortless	undemanding	fatiguing
elementary	walkover	gruelling
facile	arduous	laborious
manageable	backbreaking	onerous
painless	burdensome	strenuous
simple	complex	taxing
smooth	complicated	toilsome
straightforward	demanding	uphill

Mad Scientists

amoeba	chemistry	physics
atom	clinical studies	pipette
bacteria	data analysis	radiation
beaker	energy	samples
biology	flask	subatomic
botany	funnel	temperature
Bunsen burner	graduated cylinder	test tube
burette	laboratory	thermometer
cell	molecule	titration
centrifuge	particle	zoology

H Is For Hospital

ambulance	matron	registrar
casualty	morgue	stretcher
clinic	nurse	surgeon
clinician	operating theatre	surgery
consultant	outpatients	wheelchair
dispensary	paediatrician	
emergency	paramedic	
infection	physiotherapy	
intensive care	psychiatrist	
massage	radiologist	

Happy Endings II

acquittal
appraisal
approval
burial
confessional
deferral
denial
disapproval
dismissal
dispersal

disposal
portrayal
proposal
reappraisal
recital
refusal
rehearsal
reversal
revival
signal

survival
trial
tutorial
upheaval
withdrawal

What's Cooking?

baking
barbecuing
basting
blanching
boiling
braising
broiling
browning
caramelising
chopping

coddling
curing
dicing
fricasseeing
frying
garnishing
glazing
grating
grilling
marinating

mashing
parboiling
peeling
pickling
poaching
roasting
simmering
slicing
steaming
stewing

5-A-Day

artichoke
asparagus
aubergine
avocado
breadfruit
broccoli
butternut squash
cantaloupe
cauliflower
celeriac

courgette
cranberry
guava
kale
kiwi
kumquat
lychee
maize
mulberry
nectarine

papaya
parsley
parsnip
plantain
pomegranate
raspberry
rhubarb
shallot
spinach
tangerine

Q Is For...

quadrant
quadratic
quadruple
quaint
quake
qualms
quantum
quarter
quartered
quartz

quash
quay
queasy
quell
quench
query
quibble
quicksand
quill
quilt

quince
quip
quirk
quizzical
quota

They Asked, We Replied

admitted	exclaimed	pleaded
asked	grumbled	preached
begged	inquired	questioned
beseeched	instructed	reiterated
boasted	interrogated	repeated
bragged	interrupted	requested
commanded	lectured	responded
complained	moaned	retorted
confessed	ordered	sighed
contradicted	persisted	warned

En- The Enriched

enable	enfeeble	enslave
encapsulate	enfold	ensnare
encase	engulf	entangle
encircle	enlist	enthral
enclose	enliven	enthrone
encode	enmesh	entomb
encompass	enrapture	entrench
encrypt	enrich	entrust
endanger	enshrine	entwine
endear	enshroud	envision

Happy Endings III

betoken	laden	soften
chasten	lessen	straighten
coarsen	liken	strengthen
deaden	loosen	unburden
dishearten	madden	unfasten
embolden	moisten	
foreshorten	overburden	
hasten	reawaken	
hearken	slacken	
heighten	smoothen	

Ancient Origins

acupuncture	dire	phenomenon
affiliation	emulate	pneumonia
agrarian	epidermis	schizophrenia
anarchy	epiphany	sycophant
animosity	estuary	synthesis
authentic	fabrication	
bovine	hypocrite	
calligraphy	hypothesis	
capillary	longevity	
confidentiality	panacea	

The Age of Chivalry?

broadsword	fief	pennant
catapult	guild	pillage
chain mail	heraldry	plague
charter	jester	rampart
chivalry	joust	serf
chronicle	lance	tapestry
cloister	longbow	tournament
conquest	medieval	troubadour
falconry	moat	vassal
feudalism	parchment	villein

Bygone Days

account	documentation	record
annal	epoch	republic
antiquity	legislature	sovereign
aristocracy	memoir	testament
bourgeoisie	middle class	tyranny
chronological	monarchy	
chronology	patriarch	
civil war	peasantry	
constitution	prehistory	
democracy	rebellion	

Sound Effects

acoustic	melodic	staccato
blaring	monotonous	symphonic
cacophonous	plaintive	tumultuous
caterwauling	rattling	ululating
clattering	raucous	vibrating
discordant	resonant	
droning	rhythmic	
dulcet	ricocheting	
harmonious	riotous	
mellifluous	sonorous	

Light Effects

ablaze	flickering	lustrous
beaming	glaring	polished
blazing	gleaming	radiant
blinding	glimmering	shimmering
bright	glinting	shining
brilliant	glistening	shiny
burnished	glittering	spangling
dappled	glittery	sparkling
dazzling	luminescent	twinkling
flaring	luminous	winking

That Doesn't Look Right...

absence	convenience	hygiene
accompaniment	desperate	liaison
achievement	desperately	occasionally
acknowledgement	detached	occurrences
aggressive	diligent	opportunity
argument	existence	perseverance
average	expertise	possession
buoyant	extreme	questionnaire
communication	forwards	sincerely
consensus	government	sincerity

On The Road

bottleneck	hard shoulder	roadside rescue
breakdown	insurance	roadworks
calming	junction	roundabouts
carriageway	motorists	speed cameras
closure	motorway	speed limit
congestion	passenger	tailback
diversion	pedestrian	traffic jam
driver	pelican crossing	traffic signal
flyover	puffin crossing	warden
gridlock	roadside recovery	zebra crossing

Fasten Your Seat Belt!

accelerator	fog lights	licence plate
air conditioner	gear	rear-view mirror
airbag	hazard lights	safety belt
bonnet	headrest	splash guard
boot	high beams	spoiler
brakes	hood	steering wheel
bumper	hubcap	sunroof
chassis	ignition	windscreen
clutch	indicators	windscreen wipers
dashboard	klaxon	wing mirror

In Good Company

alliance	coven	regiment
battalion	den	scrum
bevy	diaspora	squad
brigade	enclave	syndicate
cabal	entourage	triumvirate
clique	faction	
coalition	gaggle	
cohort	legion	
congregation	mob	
coterie	posse	

From A Great Height

altitude	elevation	precipice
avalanche	foothills	range
bluff	foothold	ravine
boulder	glacier	ridges
chain	gorge	scree
chalet	mountain	sea level
cliff	mountaineer	sierra
climber	peak	slopes
crag	pinnacle	snow line
crevasse	plateau	summit

Where There's Smoke...

ash	extinct	pumice
basalt	fissure	seismograph
belching	fumes	smoky
conduit	geyser	smouldering
conical	hardening	tectonic
cooling	inactive	vent
crater	lava	volcanic
dormant	magma	volcanic rock
eruption	molten	volcano
explosion	plate	volcanoes

On Or Off The Cards?

anticipated	prospective	inconceivable
believable	reasonable	incredible
compelling	supposable	outlandish
conceivable	tenable	questionable
credible	viable	remote
feasible	doubtful	unbelievable
imaginable	dubious	unconvincing
ostensible	fanciful	unimaginable
plausible	implausible	unlikely
possible	improbable	unthinkable

Spoilt For Choice II

abundantly	fervently	outlandishly
agreeably	feverishly	paradoxically
appropriately	frenetically	reproachfully
assuredly	haphazardly	sedately
begrudgingly	incessantly	sheepishly
brutally	lamentably	spontaneously
covertly	lithely	staunchly
diligently	merely	tactfully
elusively	mildly	unpredictably
expressly	obnoxiously	vividly

Blue Rhymes With...

anthology	metre	rhyme scheme
ballad	metrical foot	rhythm
blank verse	octet	septet
couplet	ode	sonnet
elegy	poetic	stanza
epic	poetry	technique
free verse	quatrain	tercet
iambic pentameter	refrain	triplet
limerick	repetition	verse
lyric	rhyme	versification

Nessing Things Up

adeptness	foreignness	otherness
adroitness	fullness	quirkiness
aptness	haughtiness	robustness
bluntness	haziness	scantiness
callowness	indebtedness	shrewdness
comeliness	ineptness	squatness
coyness	inertness	steeliness
deftness	keenness	vastness
exactness	kindliness	wakefulness
fleetness	nothingness	weightiness

Pirates!!

- boatswain
- buccaneer
- corsair
- cutlass
- cut-throat
- double-dealing
- doubloon
- galleon
- gangplank
- gibbet
- ignominious
- infamous
- inglorious
- looting
- marauding
- musket
- mutiny
- nefarious
- notorious
- pillaging
- plundering
- privateer
- privateering
- raiding
- sacking

Well- The Well-Fed

- well-accustomed
- well-acted
- well-adapted
- well-baked
- well-befitting
- well-characterized
- well-cooked
- well-cultivated
- well-cushioned
- well-defended
- well-disciplined
- well-fashioned
- well-fed
- well-imagined
- well-inclined
- well-justified
- well-managed
- well-nourished
- well-observed
- well-paced
- well-painted
- well-placed
- well-raised
- well-received
- well-seasoned
- well-tailored
- well-taught
- well-understood
- well-ventilated
- well-washed

Ill- The Ill-Informed

ill-adjusted	ill-disposed	ill-made
ill-advised	ill-equipped	ill-mannered
ill-assorted	ill-famed	ill-matched
ill-bred	ill-fated	ill-natured
ill-chosen	ill-favoured	ill-prepared
ill-concealed	ill-fitting	ill-proportioned
ill-considered	ill-founded	ill-smelling
ill-defined	ill-gotten	ill-suited
ill-deserved	ill-humoured	ill-tempered
ill-disciplined	ill-judged	ill-timed

How Awful!

abhorrent	formidable	loathsome
abominable	frightful	nauseating
alarming	ghastly	noxious
appalling	gross	objectionable
atrocious	gruesome	odious
despicable	harrowing	repellent
detestable	heinous	repugnant
distasteful	hideous	shocking
distressing	horrendous	terrible
dreadful	horrifying	unwholesome

Measuring Up

acre	furlong	litre
bushel	gallon	megabyte
byte	gigabyte	megaton
carat	gram	milligram
cubit	hectare	millilitre
degree	inch	millimetre
dram	kilobyte	nanometre
fathom	kilogram	ounce
fluid	kilometre	pixel
foot	league	yard

And The Winner Is...

acclaim	decoration	podium
accolade	distinction	salute
applause	furnish	tribute
badge	grant	trophy
bestow	hail	vest
blue ribbon	homage	
commend	honour	
commendation	laurel	
confer	medal	
decorate	plaque	

All Shapes And Sizes

athletic	muscular	squat
awkward	nimble	stocky
buff	paunchy	sturdy
chubby	petite	sure-footed
dainty	plump	svelte
fit	rangy	tanned
graceful	rotund	trim
hulking	skinny	ungainly
lanky	slender	well-built
lithe	slim	willowy

Loanwords

al dente	fait accompli	per se
al fresco	haute cuisine	persona non grata
beaux arts	in absentia	quid pro quo
carte blanche	in loco parentis	sotto voce
compos mentis	in situ	terra firma
cordon sanitaire	laissez-faire	
de facto	mea culpa	
déjà vu	memento mori	
double entendre	par excellence	
enfant terrible	per annum	

Under-The Underlined

underachieve	underscore	underfoot
undercook	undersell	undergarment
undercut	understate	undergraduate
underestimate	undertake	underground
underfeed	underwhelm	undergrowth
undergo	underarm	underhand
underline	underbelly	underside
underpay	undercoat	understaffed
underplay	undercover	undertone
underrate	underdog	underwater

Drip...Drip...Drip

cascade	flow	saturate
condense	flush	soak
drain	gush	spill
drench	immerse	spout
dribble	inundate	spray
drip	irrigate	spurt
drizzle	leak	submerge
drown	overflow	swamp
evaporate	pour	trickle
flood	precipitate	water

GRUESOME GRAMMAR

abbreviation	demonstrative	parts of speech
apostrophe	gerund	phrasal verb
auxiliary verb	heteronym	phrase
clause	homonym	possessive
comparative	homophone	preposition
conditional	idiom	punctuation
conjugate	imperative	reflexive
conjunction	infinitive	relative
contraction	parenthesis	subordinating
co-ordinating	participle	superlative

The Silver Screen

animation	director	premiere
audience	documentary	producer
audio description	excerpt	release
auditorium	feature	scenario
biopic	footage	score
celluloid	franchise	screen
character	freeze-frame	scriptwriter
choreographer	intermission	stunt
cinema	location	subtitle
computer-generated	musical	trailer

Isn't It Crystal Clear?

ambiguous	uncertain	evident
debatable	unclear	exact
hazy	unknown	explicit
hidden	vague	intelligible
imprecise	wispy	lucid
murky	apparent	manifest
mysterious	coherent	obvious
nebulous	comprehensible	perspicuous
obscure	definite	precise
shadowy	distinct	unclouded

Friend...

accomplice	befriend	encourage
affable	bond	friend
aid	camaraderie	genial
aide	collaborator	helper
ally	companion	inseparable
amiable	companionable	jovial
amicable	comrade	partner
assist	confidant	support
assistant	cordial	supporter
associate	crony	sustain

...OR FOE?

adversary	combatant	melee
adversity	conflict	nemesis
aggression	contender	opponent
antagonist	defence	rebel
assailant	dogfight	rival
attack	encounter	saboteur
attacker	enemy	scrap
battle	foe	skirmish
challenger	foray	struggle
clash	fray	tussle

There's No Going Back

advance	endorse	progress
advocate	forge ahead	promote
approach	forward	propel
bolster	foster	push
boost	further	upraise
buttress	gain ground	
champion	improve	
cultivate	march	
drive	nourish	
elevate	proceed	

Retreat! Retreat!

abandon	flee	rout
back down	forsake	shrink
backpedal	give way	turn tail
backtrack	lose ground	vacate
capitulate	quit	withdraw
depart	recede	
disengage	recoil	
escape	retire	
evacuate	retract	
fall back	retreat	

SHERLOCK HOLMES & CO.

civilian	informer	shadowing
criminal underworld	intelligence	sleuth
deduction	investigation	surveillance
discernment	investigator	suspicion
discoveries	mafia	tailing
forensics	mobsters	testimony
gangsters	mole	victim
gumshoe	observation	villainy
implication	private eye	wiretap
informant	scout	witness

City Central

atrocity	electricity	reciprocity
audacity	ethnicity	scarcity
authenticity	felicity	simplicity
capacity	ferocity	specificity
complicity	incapacity	synchronicity
domesticity	multiplicity	tenacity
duplicity	opacity	toxicity
eccentricity	paucity	velocity
egocentricity	plasticity	veracity
elasticity	publicity	vivacity

Bookish Business

allegory	flashback	perspective
anecdote	footnotes	plagiarism
appendix	foreshadow	preface
autograph	glossary	prologue
dedication	index	prose
dictionary	legend	protagonist
encyclopaedia	myth	publication
epigraph	pagination	satire
epilogue	parody	table of contents
fable	periodical	thesaurus

Left, Right, Left, Right...

barge	mosey	toddle
career	navigate	totter
chaperone	nip	traipse
dart	prance	traverse
escort	rove	trip
flounce	scramble	troop
herd	scurry	trot
loiter	shepherd	usher
lumber	slink	waddle
meander	steal	wade

Acting Your Age

adolescent	elderly	mature
adult	fledgling	minor
aged	geriatric	naïve
babyish	girlish	senior
boyish	immature	sprightly
childish	inexperienced	spry
childlike	infantile	teenage
decrepit	innocent	vigorous
developing	junior	well-preserved
doddering	juvenile	youthful

Un- The Unheeded

unbiased	unequal	unravel
unbidden	unerring	unrivalled
unbridled	unfold	unruly
uncanny	unfounded	unsavoury
uncharted	unfurl	unscathed
unchecked	unheeded	unseemly
uncommon	unhinged	unsuited
uncouth	unleash	untapped
unduly	unnamed	unveil
unearth	unnerve	unwieldy

The Big Top

acrobatics	hippodrome	somersault
admission	human cannonball	spectators
antics	juggler	stilts
audacious	knife-thrower	strongman
carnival	lion-tamer	sword-swallower
Cirque du Soleil	parade	tightrope
clown	ringmaster	trampoline
death-defying	sequins	trapeze
fascination	sideshow	troupe
fire-eater	snake charmer	unicycle

Dotting I's & Crossing T's

annotate	marginalia	script
communicate	margins	signature
compose	penmanship	squiggle
correspond	redraft	succinct
couch	rewrite	terminology
cursive	salutation	transcribe
formulate	scratch	typewriting
handwriting	scrawl	typing
jot	scribble	verbalise
longhand	scribe	verbose

What's It Worth?

cherished	profitable	inferior
costly	rare	insignificant
esteemed	substantial	modest
expensive	treasured	paltry
exquisite	valuable	petty
inestimable	cheap	tawdry
irreplaceable	contemptible	trashy
laudable	debased	trifling
priceless	good-for-nothing	trivial
prized	inconsequential	valueless

Open For Business

auctioneer	personal shopper	trader
cashier	retailer	tradesman
dealer	sales assistant	trafficker
distributor	salesman	vendor
ebayer	salesperson	wholesaler
hawker	scrap dealer	
licensee	seller	
merchant	shopkeeper	
packer	stallholder	
peddler	supplier	

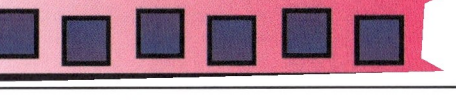

'Ch' Is For 'Chaos'

ache	cholera	ochre
alchemy	choral	orchid
anchored	chord	psyche
archaic	chorister	schema
archive	chorus	scheme
chaotic	chromatic	schism
chasm	chrome	scholarly
chemical	chronic	schooling
chemotherapy	echo	technology
chimera	hierarchy	trachea

On The Face Of It

animated	fresh-faced	profile
ashen	furrowed	scarred
blotchy	glowering	scrubbed
bronzed	grimace	snub-nosed
chiselled	hatchet-faced	squinting
countenance	hawkish	swollen
craggy	jowl	visage
deadpan	leathery	weather-beaten
dimpled	made-up	wincing
expressionless	pallid	wrinkled

Art For Art's Sake

canvas	gallery	pastel
cartoon	gouache	picture
charcoal	graffiti	portrait
clay	kiln	pose
crayon	masterpiece	pottery
design	mould	sculptor
draw	mural	sculpture
easel	oils	sketch
exhibition	paint	watercolour
fresco	palette	wheel

A Splash Of Colour

bleached	flamboyant	multicoloured
brash	flaming	muted
chintzy	fluorescent	neutral
colourless	glowing	opalescent
co-ordinated	iridescent	restrained
dappled	jazzy	sombre
discoloured	matching	tinged
dusty	mellow	tinted
festive	monochrome	translucent
fiery	monotone	vibrant

Out- The Outnumbered

outbreak	outlast	output
outburst	outlaw	outrank
outcast	outlier	outreach
outclass	outlive	outskirts
outcome	outmanoeuvre	outsource
outcry	outnumber	outstay
outdo	outpace	outstretch
outflank	outperform	outstrip
outgrow	outplay	outweigh
outgun	outpouring	outwit

Upstairs & Downstairs

attic	eaves	lounge
balcony	entrance hall	nursery
basement	foyer	pantry
breakfast bar	garage	parlour
breakfast room	garret	scullery
cellar	hallway	skylight
chimney	kitchen	solarium
conservatory	larder	studio
dining room	laundry room	study
drawing room	lobby	suite

Bad Hair Day?

abundant	flowing	receding
bald	frizzy	shaggy
balding	glossy	spiky
barber	greasy	swept-back
bristly	hairdresser	thinning
bushy	hairline	tousled
buzz cut	lank	unkempt
close-cropped	luxuriant	wavy
coiffed	matted	wind-blown
crew cut	permed	windswept

Player 1 Is Ready

arcade	emulator	platform
artificial intelligence	family-oriented	playable
avatar	game engine	professional
beginner	gamepad	quest
cheat mode	gamer	role-playing game
console	graphics	shoot-'em-up
controller	handheld	single-player
demo	interface	split screen
downloadable	joypad	virtual reality
driving simulator	multiplayer	visual effects

That's A Proper Word?!

agog	didgeridoo	hippocampus
akimbo	doldrums	hogwash
amok	dunderhead	huzzah
balderdash	earwig	ignoramus
bamboozle	fandango	indomitable
bedlam	fez	interloper
cahoots	fiddlesticks	ironclad
caterwaul	genteel	jalopy
contraband	gizmo	jamboree
desperado	heyday	junket

INDEX

ENGLISH LANGUAGE CURRICULUM-BASED WORDS
Collective Nouns (p. 18)

Commonly Mistaken Spellings (p. 17)

Compound Words
Hyphenated Adjectives: ill- (p. 23)
Hyphenated Adjectives: well- (p. 22)

Doubled Consonants (p. 5)

Grammatical Terms (p. 27)

Letter String 'ch' as 'k' (p. 35)

Prefixes
de- (p. 8)
en- (p. 13)
out- (p. 37)
un- (p. 33)
under- (p. 26)

Suffixes
-age (p. 6)
-al (p. 11)
-en (p. 14)

Words Beginning with 'q' (p. 12)

Word Building
-city (p. 31)
-ness (p. 21)

ENGLISH LITERATURE CURRICULUM-BASED WORDS
Books (p. 31)
Common Shakespearean Words (p. 5)
Poetry (p. 21)

Words from Other Languages
Greek & Latin Origins (p. 14)
Loanwords (p. 25)

GENERAL KNOWLEDGE WORDS
Art (p. 36)
Awards (p. 24)
Car Parts (p. 18)
Chemical Elements (p. 6)
Cinema & Film (p. 27)
Circus, The (p. 33)
Detectives (p. 30)
Enmity (p. 29)
Food Preparation (p. 11)
Friendship (p. 28)
Fruit & Vegetables (p. 12)
Hospital, The (p. 10)
Hunting & Hunters (p. 9)
Laboratory, The (p. 10)
Metals & Alloys (p. 7)
Middle Ages, The (p. 15)
Mountains (p. 19)
Past, The (p. 15)
Pirates (p. 22)
Road Traffic (p. 17)
Rooms in a House (p. 38)
Sellers (p. 35)
Video Games (p. 39)
Volcanoes (p. 19)
Water (p. 26)
Weights & Measures (p. 24)
Writing (p. 34)

ANTONYM PAIRS
Clear vs Unclear (p. 28)
Easy vs Hard (p. 9)
Likely vs Unlikely (p. 20)
Valued vs Worthless (p. 34)

SYNONYMS
Awful (p. 23)
Moving Backwards (p. 30)
Moving Forwards (p. 29)
Said (p. 13)
Silly (p. 7)
Walk (p. 32)

CREATIVE WRITING WORDS
Fun Words (p. 39)

Mixed Adjectives (p. 8)

Mixed Adverbs (p. 20)

Targeted
Age (p. 32)
Colours (p. 37)
Face, The (p. 36)
Hair (p. 38)
Light (p. 16)
Physical Traits (p. 25)
Sounds (p. 16)

Printed in Great Britain
by Amazon